This book belongs to:

....

Rum & Coke
on the Rocks

Teresa Gard

Written by Teresa Gard
www.teresagard.co.uk

Illustrations by Deborah Partington
info@deborahpartington.co.uk

Designed by David Merrifield
david@themerrifields.com

First published by Teresa Gard, 2012
© 2012 Teresa Gard.

Further writing by the author can be found at
http://valleygardenparadise.blogspot.com

Printed in England by St Andrew's Press of Wells.
All proceeds from the sale of this book will go to charity.

"Our perfect companions
never have fewer than four feet."

Sidonie-Gabrielle Colette, 1873 - 1954

For my husband Will. With love and thanks

"Jack and Molly inhabited different worlds, until serendipity fused their paths. Pathologically private, Jack's life was punctuated by shadow and suspicion. A man alone, he lived vicariously, passing unnoticed amongst life's outsiders."

That's how Jack's obituary might have read when I first met him. Allow me to introduce myself. I'm Coke, the sniffer dog, named in honour of the white stuff. My relationship with Jack was business; we met on the job. Working side by side, I had the opportunity to observe Jack intimately. I knew when he was nervous from the tic in his cheek and a salty heat that emanated from his palms. We spoke the same silent language; smells, symbols, and gut feelings. The force was our vocation, we were born to it, both loving the thrill of the chase, the scent of the prize.

When we were not working, we lived in Jack's Victorian terrace on Foxton Road, overlooking Vauxhall Park. In the evening, after a shower, Jack liked to relax by listening to opera, smoke from a habanos shrouding him in a veil. As Carmen's spirit electrified the room, the muslin curtains would billow on the breeze behind his head. Stretched out on my sheepskin I could study him in profile; black-rimmed glasses perched on high cheekbones, an aquiline nose accentuated by a severe crew cut. Jack's off-duty uniform was always a black turtleneck and jeans; the conformity provided anonymity. When we went undercover he would allow his hair to grow. Then, curls softened his features and contact lenses revealed cobalt pools framed by Clarke Gable brows.

On the mantelpiece there was a photo of a young woman surrounded by star fruit, papaya and cherries, her head thrown back in laughter. This was Jack's late mother, in the 1970s, when she ran a fruit and veg stall in Berwick Street. Emotionally he went to the grave with her. He was fifteen when she died. Sometimes, as the vibration of *Toreador* reached its crescendo, Jack's repressed spirit would break free. Unaware, he would lose himself, his hands soaring on imaginary thermals like an eagle on the wing. Of course, I was the only soul privy to this transformation. As soon as we returned to regular duties he would visit Sweeney Todd in Balham and within minutes his troubadour's spirit would be carpeting the linoleum, all external expression of sentiment neutralised.

One Friday, emerging like caged miners from the Drain at Waterloo, Jack and I decided to follow the river home along the South Bank. I spotted her first. Sporting a cherry cloche, she was running a rolled newspaper along the railings, an impish smile on her lips. She stopped and acknowledged me: "What a handsome dog!" Then looking at Jack, "Do you mind if I stroke him?" As she spoke, the lead tightened around my neck, almost choking me; the result of Jack's response reflex as he winced at her open manner. I had to hand it to him though, he was a pro; the tone of his voice did not betray his feelings.

"Okay love, go ahead," he replied casually. Her eyes widened in surprise. I had seen this reaction before. His voice was disarming, mellow with the resonance of a six litre Bentley, always a surprise from the mouth of this Invisible Man. She bent down and smoothed my ears, her velvet gloves infused with vanilla. I was in heaven. It must be the way you humans feel when you eat chocolate.

"What's his name?"

"Coke."

"What a great name. I must admit I'm partial to rum and coke myself." Her singsong words soothed my ears and ice cream rippled down my spine. I wasn't the only one affected; Jack started to thaw.

"Hello Coke, I'm Molly," she purred. "I couldn't help noticing how beautifully you walk with your master. What a well behaved doggie you are!"

A rhythmic pulse ricocheted down the lead. Momentarily distracted from my compliment I looked up to confirm the sensation... yes, as I had suspected, Jack was trying not to smile. Molly was oblivious.

"So Coke, is this your regular walk?"

I applied imperceptible pressure upwards to focus Jack's attention and stimulate his vocal chords.

"Yes, we live over the bridge near the park."

"So do I. How strange," she mused. "I walk this way every day. I've never seen you before." Her voice lowered as she crouched down to my level and confided, "You know, I really miss my dog now that I live in London." I noticed that a stray golden curl had escaped from her hat. I just love blondes.

"In fact, Coke here is my partner," Jack volunteered. My ears shot up in salute. Sensing an opportunity, I cocked my head to the right to catch his eye. Objective achieved, I then stared at him very hard, willing him to go on. This was

our weekend off; I wanted him to ask her to come out with us. Molly was already on my wavelength.

"I know this sounds cheeky, but would you mind if I joined you and Coke for a walk sometime?"

Great! I knew this was our chance; Jack had to go for it. I held my breath. Electricity danced in the air, pirouetting along my whiskers and making my tail spin. Then, like gunshots, staccato words shot from Jack's mouth. "How about… meeting us here. At two o'clock. Tomorrow. For a walk. Along the river?"

Molly's face glowed pale rose. "I would love to. See you tomorrow, Coke." I smiled back with my ears slightly elevated; it was the matinée idol pose that I had perfected for my licence!

The following afternoon a cursory glance at my reflection in a café window revealed sculpted muscles rippling under my haematite coat. I accessorised with a cranberry collar and lead. I must say I was chuffed with the result, a canine Rupert Everett, you know; that certain *je ne sais quoi*? For me it had been love at first sight. After our walk we sat on a riverside bench outside a brasserie. I couldn't resist putting my paws up onto the seat and kissing her cheek. Caddish, I know, but being a dog has its advantages. My experience was interrupted by Jack's growl, "Coke, down boy!"

Molly hugged me. "What an attentive date!" she laughed.

Jack relaxed with Molly, the scythes etched around his mouth receded and his eyes crinkled like tissue paper when she dueted *little ol' wine drinker* me with Dino, and teased him about upgrading his pint of Newcastle Brown to a glass of Pinot.

Six months later we all moved into a cellared townhouse, part of an old winery. Jack explained to me that it had once been the hub of merchant trade in

Victorian London. I got heady on mould spores lurking in the tunnels as we investigated the ancient oak casks. Leather chairs impregnated with tobacco and sweat in the Houses of Parliament had introduced me to history. The walled gardens contained an eight acre cemetery built to accommodate the victims of Asiatic cholera.

When our off-duty coincided with Molly's day off, she would take me exploring. In her other life she was a goldsmith, setting precious gem-stones into handcrafted jewellery. We followed the trail of Jack The Ripper and visited Billingsgate fish market, sensory heaven. I could always tell her days off; she would pad around in her pyjamas and tend her orchids, before pulling on her boots saying, "Come on, Coke, let's go and see our friends in the cemetery." We were getting to know them, discovering their stories; it was a different kind of detective work. As the sun stretched through the oak trees, we would crunch along the path to the Garden of Rest. Inside, marble, stone and teak monuments in various states of disrepair punctuated the landscape. Moss and decaying bindweed mulched the ground; sometimes I would spiral into frenzied barking as the fumes of a discarded hypodermic needle alerted me to danger. Molly would read the inscriptions out loud to me:

"HENRY JACK ROWE, 1897 to 1917."

His monument was a broken pillar. "That symbolises a life cut short," she sighed. "He was only twenty years old; he must have died in the Great War. So much promise, his whole life ahead of him." His brother Michael lay next to him under a covered urn, 1896-1915.

I began to understand a life cut short. I loved my work with Jack; it was all I had ever known but everything started to change. Our lives turned upside down. Jack and I came home one morning after a night shift at Wandsworth. He stood awkwardly by the toaster, and then, as the clock chimed; he perched on the edge of the rocking chair.

"Molly, I got a letter yesterday. Coke's got to retire at the end of October." I couldn't believe my ears; I must have heard him wrong. I was at the top of my game, a seasoned pro! My specialty was sniffing out drugs that had been mailed to the prisoners inside radios and other gifts. I had just received an award for the most finds. Oh yes, I understood a life cut short. Molly pleaded with Jack to adopt me.

"Molly, I've always known that this time would come; my relationship with Coke is business." He paused, studying his neat fingernails. "There's something else... I'm going undercover for six months."

"You're doing what? Why? Just pretending that the last few months never happened?"

Thunderous tension consumed the room; it was explosive. I lay motionless in my basket, just like Half-Pillar in his grave.

My only option was to listen, to watch through my lashes; it played out like a scene from a grainy old black and white movie. At first Molly just shook her head. "You can't just disappear... abandon us?" Unwelcome tears choked her breathing. She was proud; I knew that for Molly crying was not an option.

"Molly, it's the way my life is, the way it's always been. I've always told you that I'm better on my own." An eerie silence filled the space; his admission stopped time in its tracks. We had been having so much fun, why did Jack have to spoil everything now? I loved our picnics in Hyde Park on Sunday afternoons. It felt like Groundhog Day, only this time I couldn't go back to my old life with him.

As Jack began to inhabit his new persona he withdrew. The changes were subtle at first; he lost interest in our daily activities. He stopped asking Molly about the gemstone couriers from Pakistan touting star rubies and sapphires with their stories of life on the Silk Road, and our investigations concerning Half-Pillar, Covered-Urn and their comrades. Instead he engaged silently with the TV remote. Surfing the channels, he slowly evaporated into the ether. It was as if a cloak of depression had devoured him. Once more he was invisible.

Jack left a void in our lives. Molly masked her sadness to the outside world; it was only at night, under the cover of darkness, that she let the floodgates open. By day she reverted to auto-pilot, numbing herself with practicalities.

She applied to the Police to adopt me, and to ensure that we met the criteria she changed her working routine. We created a design studio in the spare room so that we could work from home three days a week. I enjoyed being back in partnership! But it was only part-time; I couldn't go out to work with her in Hatton Garden. The other days I had to stay at home alone. The tedium was suffocating, all the energy that my job had demanded turned in on itself. I felt that I was on the

scrap heap; I missed the camaraderie and routine of the Force. When Molly went to the

workshop she left the radio on to keep me company. I learned a lot, lying on the sofa,

listening to *Woman's Hour*. Jenni Murray discussed the pitfalls of not planning properly

for retirement. If I'd had a voice I would have phoned in; I had plenty to say on the

subject. My only respite was Molly's day off. Wednesdays smelled different; roasted

coffee beans and toast infused the hallway.

One May morning we set off as usual. The gravel was ribboned with bluebells and

wild garlic. From a distance we noticed that something was tied to the gate with blue

nylon rope.

**GARDEN CLOSED TO THE PUBLIC UNTIL
FURTHER NOTICE. SITE UNSAFE**

A padlock blocked our entry. We pressed our faces against the rusting bars straining for a glimpse of Half-Pillar. Molly, her knuckles raised like the tombstones, rattled the gate in frustration. Unsolicited tears splashed onto my nose. "Oh Coke, what's happening to us? First you get early retirement, then Jack vaporises and now this." Kissing my wet nose, she snuffled "Come on. Let's go to Vincenzo's."

My ears pricked up and my tail helicoptered. Vincenzo sold ice cream, and I loved ice cream. We dogs are very different from our people; we live in the moment. I kept in step with Molly, trying to adopt the required disheartened demeanor. Dutifully looking up to check that she was okay, I tried to contain my excitement.

Vincenzo's was on the other side of the Albert Bridge. Red chequered cloths fluttered above the cobblestones as Vincenzo glided between the tables, trays of coffee and speciality ices perched on three fingers. When he welcomed his customers, malteser eyes submerged into his ample cheeks. "Molly, Coke...

Ciao! What can I get for you today?"

"Two mocha ice creams and a plate of crispy bacon, please."

Molly looked sternly at me; I was drooling!

The shrewd Neapolitan studied Molly. Her aquamarine eyes were ringed red. "You look sad today, what's the matter?"

"Oh Vincenzo, I don't know. Everything is changing so fast. It's the end of an era."

Vincenzo perched his notepad on his belly. He said nothing, simply raised his brows. "We've just come from the old cemetery; they've locked the gate and closed it to the public. I can't believe it! Apart from your gelati, it was our only refuge from the madness of this metropolis."

"I'm so sorry to 'ear that. Give me a minute. Let me get your ice cream. It's my Papa's special recipe; it will soothe your soul."

I whined and thumped my tail on the pavement, I knew it was a crisis but I was being ignored.

"Si si, Signor Coke, momentito. Your bacon is a coming. I haven't forgotten. Crispy, jus' how you like it!" I wasn't sure whether to start with the ice cream or the bacon, or maybe if Molly was distracted I would be able to eat both together. Now that would be a perfect combo. I looked up at Molly, drool framing my mouth like a Mexican's moustache. It made her smile. Vincenzo pulled out a chair. Resting his chin on a tripod of fingers he studied Molly. "Maybe you need a change of scene?" he ventured.

"You are right, Vincenzo. You know what? I'd like to start again. I'd like to go to my uncle's beach house in Cornwall; he left it to me in his will. When I was at school I beachcombed with him all summer. The sun and sea salt baked my skin and spun my hair like candy floss." Vincenzo nodded, gently coaxing her to continue.

"I'd spend every day on the beach scavenging among the rocks for treasure. That's where it all started, my fascination with gemstones and fossils."

"So what's stopping you?"

"The obvious, of course," she replied, I thought a little petulantly. "What stops most of us living our dreams? I have to earn a living."

At that moment one of the yummy-mummies shrieked across her Prada pram, "Yoo-hoo, Vincenzo, two skinny lattes on ice please. Lots of ice."

Vincenzo winked at me. "Jus' a moment, I'll be back."

The Yummies placated, he returned, placing two small glasses of limoncello on our table. "Molly, listen, I have a crazy idea, but hey it might jus' work." We followed his gaze as he pointed down the road. Wedged in between a Mini and a moped there was an old ice cream van. "I've just inherited my papa's old *gelateria su ruote*; it arrived las' week from Napoli." His chest inflated with pride.

"Why don't you borrow it for the summer and sell my ices on the beach?"

Molly's eyes were fixed on the van. I grabbed my moment. In an instant I had swallowed both my bacon and mocha ice cream, cool and crunchy with a smoky aftertaste, delicious! My opportunism bypassed Molly, her gaze still fixed on Vincenzo who continued, "I've got Papa's *Bibbia* with all his recipes. It would help you, and it would sure help me."

Six weeks later Molly and I were travelling in the lilac ice cream van emblazoned with purple psychedelic writing advertising our wares:

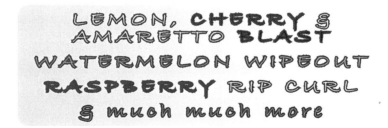

LEMON, CHERRY & AMARETTO BLAST
WATERMELON WIPEOUT
RASPBERRY RIP CURL
& much much more

Right from the start I loved life on the road. As co-pilot I was allowed to lean out of the window, my ears flapping in the breeze. We listened to Planet Rock instead of Radio Four; my harmonising with Molly's Beach Boys melody was awesome. The monochrome fog of London gave way to winding roads with hints of manure and ozone. So much better than travelling on the tube.

Uncle John's cottage was built into the cliff above a waterfall that plunged onto a shingle beach below. Molly introduced me to the delights of the coastal path and taught me to dive into the waves as she spun stones. We took up boogie boarding… hey dude… what a thrill! I loved to paddle out into the surf up to my chin before catching a wave back to the beach to wait for Molly. We made a perfect couple, the Fred and Ginger of the beach: she was blonde and beautiful, and I was dark and agile. We owned that shoreline!

My new scent of choice was neoprene; just a whiff sent me into a frenzy. Sometimes I followed the wrong wetsuit up the beach; we dogs don't see colour, to me every wetsuit had the scent of Molly. I learned to bounce on my paws like a ballerina to beg for another go. It made Molly laugh. She looked even more beautiful when the sun baked the sea salt into a crystal halo; she really was my guardian angel.

When the tide was too far out for surfing I would nip into the old sea pool to freshen up. If I was quick I could be in and out in a flash before the lifeguards noticed me; if not they would shout out over the loudspeaker. I would scramble out of the far side and shake myself dry on the sea wall, gazing across at Barrel Rock with a nonchalant air. Shaken but not stirred, I would acknowledge them with a brisk wag of my tail. Life on the beach was cool.

Each morning we parked the van at the edge of the sand, our Neapolitan melodies surfing the airwaves from rooftop speakers. We seduced the bathers' taste buds with the promise of:

ROCK POOL DE MENTHE

ORANGE & LIME ZEST BREAK

and **SLOE SUNSET SPECTACULAR**.

At night, as Molly experimented and adapted recipes from *la Bibbia di Gelati di Massimo* in the clifftop kitchen, I would lie patiently on the cool flags, ever hopeful of catching a stray slice of melon or banana. In fact, ever hopeful of a slice of anything, I became a great catch; focused and fast. My tummy gurgled as I kept it topped up with mouthwatering treats. I was in heaven. Long summer days and retirement merged seamlessly.

One evening, as the beach was clearing after a busy day, I was dozing on my rug outside the van while Molly relaxed in her deckchair. My nostrils caught a soft thermal and twitched in recognition of a familiar scent on the air. I looked up into the sun and saw a man silhouetted against the white stone of the lifeguard station.

His curly hair was moving with the wind; a guitar strapped across his back. I cocked my head to one side and whimpered as he approached us.

"Coke, what's the matter?" Molly asked, looking up.

"Hello, Molly. Hello, Coke. So this is where you've been hiding." The shadow studied the menu. "I'll try a *Tumultuous Tangerine Tunnel Twister*." Baritone notes melted his vowels.

"Jack! What are you doing here?"

"Melons and cherries remind me of Saturdays on the stall with Mum," he smiled, looking at the tropical fruit motifs on our van, "I've come for the jazz festival. I've been travelling for a couple of months now."

"Are you still undercover?" Molly avoided his gaze, reaching down to stroke my ears. Her hand was shaking. It smelled of salt.

"No. Not now. After I left you, I realised what a mistake I'd made." I nuzzled

Molly's hand, pushing her arm up into the cuddle position. "You and Coke are the best things that ever happened to me." I nudged her again as we waited to hear more. "I decided that it was time to disengage my self-destruct button. Time to move on." His voice cracked as he looked out towards the horizon. "You and Coke brought the colour back into my life, Molly."

"What about your job? The Force is your life."

"When I joined, it was real policing. Now, when they give you a case they just want you to turn on the computer and open a spreadsheet. That's not me, so I've jacked it all in. I thought I'd give life a chance."

Molly buried her face in my ears. It took time for his words to sink in. Looking down she noticed a white three-legged terrier standing beside him. "Who's your friend?"

"Oh, this is Rum. I found her in an alleyway in Soho, chucked out with the rubbish. She's like me... damaged goods. But I was hoping you'd give us a chance."

I waited for a sign from Molly, an indication of how she wanted to play it. I waited and waited, until a fleeting twitch released the tension on her forehead. Her shoulders dropped, she let out a deep sigh. I recognised my cue.

With the youthful athleticism of the surfer I had become, I sprang up from my rug and offered Jack a high five. Glancing coyly at Rum I lowered my chest and rested on my front paws, a playful gesture of welcome. She reciprocated. Retirement was definitely looking up!

A story inspired by Zeus

CREEED

Zeus, 2004-2011

Cornish born and bred, Zeus was our perfect companion. Born the summer of the Athens Olympics, he lived as a kennel dog for a year until we were introduced to him. He arrived on Maundy Thursday and immediately earned the first of his many nicknames; *Dodger*, as in *The Artful*, for Zeus was a food thief extraordinaire! It is impossible to count the times that cheese for an omelette disappeared into his tummy before reaching the pan.

From day one he was a wonderful dog; gentle, knowing and aloof. Our Sun God loved to sunbathe on top of the patio table, keeping a watchful eye on his territory. Don't be deceived, however, he was also a brilliant gun dog; calm, focused and born to work.

True to his breed Zeus adored the water. An experienced surfer, he was fearless in the north Cornish surf. Without hesitation he would dive through the waves to retrieve his ball, emerging in a halo of salt, eyes wide with anticipation and prancing on his front paws he would ask for another go. If the tide was out he would plunge into the sea pool without a care before the lifeguards had a chance to admonish him over the loudspeaker.

On the last day of November 2011 it became clear that something was very wrong with Zeus. In contrast to the intrepid ball chaser of the previous day, he refused to go for his walk or eat his supper. Instead he stared at us - his way of asking for help. Emergency blood tests revealed that he was anaemic with an auto-immune disorder; his platelets and red blood cells were being destroyed. He was referred as an emergency to The Small Animal Hospital for investigations and a blood transfusion.

Zeus accepted his stay in intensive care with calm stoicism. From the outset he was treated with kindness and respect by Christina Maunder and her dedicated team. He was given his own consulting room every afternoon to receive visitors, and even allowed up onto a make-shift sofa wrapped in his Dad's fleece. He admitted to us that there were in fact several benefits to being in hospital; being surrounded by pretty nurses intent on spoiling him with cuddles, and the opportunity to chew the cud in the evenings with the student vets before lights out.

He learned to order fresh chicken for every meal: "It's simple," he would say. "I just turn my head away in disgust at anything less."

Over the following two weeks Zeus received two blood transfusions. Despite state-of-the-art medication his blood continued to clot and he developed thromboembolic disease with a pulmonary clot that affected his breathing. He never stopped trying to surmount his difficulties, accepting an oxygen mask and catheters in his legs without complaint. We witnessed first-hand the dedication, kindness and professionalism of all the staff in the intensive care unit. It was with very heavy hearts that together with the medical team we decided, in view of his deteriorating quality of life, to discontinue his treatment and let him come home for one last day. Zeus was just seven years old.

On the morning of 14 December, Christina ensured that everything was in place for Zeus' discharge. As we were leaving he stopped and turned back to Christina to say thank you and goodbye; as always a perfect gentleman. It was a telling moment.

His tail helicoptered with delight when he arrived home and our other dogs welcomed him with a sniff and a kiss. We turned all the clocks to the wall; time stood still as we enjoyed our Christmas Day with Zeus. He feasted on pea and ham soup and left-over Chinese take-away in front of the aga while Elvis serenaded him with Christmas carols. Surrounded by his family and favourite teddies, Zeus slipped away just after 3pm as the sun began to set. Through our tears we heard the song,

"Hark the herald angels sing, glory to the new-born King". Our Sun God had arrived in heaven to surf with the angels.

A story inspired by Zeus

My favourite charities

My favourite charities

This book was written, in part, to commemorate the life of our lovely dog, Zeus, but I wrote it principally to raise funds for two charities that are very dear to my heart...

The Langford Trust
for Animal Health and Welfare

I am fortunate to live just a few miles from the world renowned University of Bristol School of Veterinary Science in North Somerset. Their Small Animal Hospital is where Zeus was cared for during his last days.

The Langford Trust for Animal Health and Welfare was founded in 1990 to support the expansion of facilities at the hospital for the education of veterinary surgeons and the treatment of sick and injured animals. The Trust's main objective is to relieve suffering and to further animal welfare, and to achieve this, their policy is to support the vet school through long term investment in the students who perfect their life-saving skills under tuition from Langford's top surgical teams, and through the provision of funding for equipment and clinical facilities (for the diagnosis and treatment of the thousands of patients brought to Langford each year).

Two new state of the art hospital facilities have recently been opened by the Trust's Patron, the Duchess of Cornwall. The new small animal surgery building has excellent anaesthesia facilities, modern imaging suites for CT, Xray and ultra sound, specialist operating theatres and a large, superlative intensive care unit. Zeus was the first patient to receive treatment. The new large animal surgery boasts a specialist orthopaedic theatre, a general surgical theatre and a standing surgery facility. The Trust's small and large patients will not be the only beneficiaries of these tremendous new facilities - the surgeons and students who work and learn there will also benefit.

The Langford Trust continues to raise funds to support more clinical research to benefit cats and dogs, and plans to build a standing Magnetic Resonance Imaging (MRI) facility for horses.

The work of the Langford Trust for Animal Health and Welfare

Bude Sea Pool, c.1930

Friends of
Bude Sea Pool

Bude lies on the northern Cornish coast, and for many years we have escaped the hustle and bustle of everyday life to this beautiful and tranquil part of Cornwall. It was a particular favourite of Zeus.

The magnificent sea pool was constructed in 1929, and has provided a thrilling and entertaining venue for holiday-makers and locals ever since, being topped up by the refreshing Atlantic Ocean twice a day. On a summer's day the sprawling, sparkling expanse of the Sea Pool offers an idyllic opportunity to laze, play or bathe in calm sea water.

The Sea Pool was threatened with closure in 2010 when Cornwall Council finally decided it could no longer afford to manage and maintain it. The Friends of Bude Sea

Pool was formed in 2011 by a group of local residents and volunteers, eager to preserve their special Sea Pool and protect it from closure and possible demolition. Within months, the Friends had generated enough support and initial funding to take over the running of the Sea Pool.

Today, the charity takes care of all staffing, repairs and maintenance of the Sea Pool, and relies on membership fees, donations, business sponsorship, grant funding and goodwill to keep the Sea Pool open.

Photo: Tim Martindale